Newspapers

From Start to Finish

Mindi Rose Englart
Photographs by Jeff Sobiech

BLACKBIRCH PRESS, INC.
WOODBRIDGE, CONNECTICUT

For Shayna Leah Roffman

Special Thanks
The author and the publisher would like to thank Kathy Andrews, Ken DeLisa, and the Hartford Courant staff for their generous help in putting this project together.

If you would like more information about Hartford's Camp Courant, the nation's largest free day camp, visit the Camp web site at www.campcourant.org

Published by Blackbirch Press, Inc.
260 Amity Road
Woodbridge, CT 06525

e-mail: staff@blackbirch.com

Web site: www.blackbirch.com

©2001 by Blackbirch Press, Inc.
First Edition

Printed in the United States

10 9 8 7 6 5 4 3 2 1

Photo Credits: All photographs ©Jeff Sobiech. Cover photos by Bruce Glassman and Jeff Sobiech.

Library of Congress Cataloging-in-Publication Data
Englart, Mindi Rose
Newspapers: from start to finish / by Mindi Rose Englart.
       p.   cm.
Includes index.
Summary: Describes how newspapers are made.
     ISBN 1-56711-484-9 (alk. paper)
1. Newspapers—Juvenile literature. [1. Newspapers.] I. Title.
PN4776 .E495 2001
070.1'72—dc21   2001002366

Contents

What is black and white (and yellow and blue) and read all over? Newspapers, of course! Newspapers have been around for centuries. All around the world, they provide news and information to people just like you.

Today, newspapers are published in almost every country. Over 55 million newspapers are purchased in America every day.

A daily newspaper office is never closed. Employees work 24 hours a day, 365 days a year! With so much to report every day, how do newspapers get made?

Stacks of newspapers about to be bundled for delivery.

Excellence in Journalism

The Hartford Courant is the oldest continuously published newspaper in America. Each day, The Courant prints between 200,000 and 350,000 newspapers. That's nearly 74 million newspapers a year!

The Courant publishes a mix of local, national, and international news. The newspaper has won two Pulitzer prizes—the highest award in journalism.

*Above: Pulitzer Prize. **Right:** The Hartford Courant building. **Far right:** A security officer welcomes visitors.*

4

It All Starts With a Story

Think of all the news events that happen around the world each day. With so many stories to choose from, who decides what will appear in your local paper? Every day, the managing editor meets with editors (managers) of all the news departments at 10 A.M. and again at 4 P.M. The editors share story ideas they've gotten through press releases, phone calls, the Internet, and other news services. The managing editor picks the stories that will appear in the next day's paper.

SAT 3/10
SUN 3/11
MON 3/12
MISSINGKIDS 3/25-4/1
BIPOLAR
FIGHTER
TOWNTRIBE
HALE
TAXGAMBLE
CANCERKIDS
ERRORS
CENSUS
Refer to Northeast
Refer to NCAA Selection
NCAA Tournaments
Men-March15-April
Women-March16-April 1
FRI 3/16
SAT 3/17
SUN
MON

Opposite: *The chief editor (behind desk) discusses story ideas with the Sunday magazine editor.* ***Inset:*** *Mail and phone calls about possible stories come to the message desk, where they are delivered to reporters and editors.* ***Above:*** *The managing editor writes the weekly front page story possibilities on a board.* ***Right:*** *Editors gather for the 10 A.M. news meeting.*

Assignments

After the news meeting, each department editor talks with his or her staff. News editors assign stories to reporters. Photo editors assign pictures to photojournalists. Graphic design editors assign illustrations, maps, charts, and diagrams to artists.

Above: *A graphic designer looks at yesterday's paper to see how her illustration looks in print.* **Left:** *An editor and reporter at work.*

A sports reporter covers a high school basketball game.

Getting "the Scoop"

It is the reporter's job to find out the details of a story. For a sports story, a reporter may go to a high school basketball game. Afterwards, the reporter may interview the team coaches, the fans, and the winning and losing team members. These people's comments may be included in the story.

A Picture's Worth a Thousand Words

While the reporter collects information for the story, the photojournalist takes pictures. A photojournalist must keep an eye on the action at all times. He or she doesn't want to miss an important shot.

The photojournalist must be aware of lighting, color, and movement—to make sure a photo is clear and effective. The photojournalist may shoot hundreds of photographs in order to get one or two that will appear in the paper.

A photojournalist shoots pictures to go with a sports story.

Writing and Filing a Story

After collecting all the facts and quotes, a reporter often goes back to the newsroom to write an article.

Sometimes a reporter uses a laptop computer to write a story as it happens. When the story is finished, the reporter sends it electronically to an editor at The Courant. This electronic method saves valuable time. The later a story is handed in, the faster people in other departments have to work to get the paper out in time.

A sports reporter uses a laptop computer to electronically send a finished story to the newsroom for editing.

The photo editor uses a lupe (special magnifying glass) to look over the photojournalist's negatives to help pick the best shots.

Preparing the Photo

A photojournalist returns to the newsroom to develop film. Then he or she meets with the photo editor, who helps to pick the best shot. The photojournalist fine-tunes the best selections, using a special computer program to change color and other details.

13

Older Than the Nation

When the United States became a nation in 1776, The Hartford Courant *(then* The Connecticut Courant*), was already 12 years old. The Courant is the largest daily paper in Connecticut—with a daily circulation of 202,914 and a Sunday circulation of 293,221.*

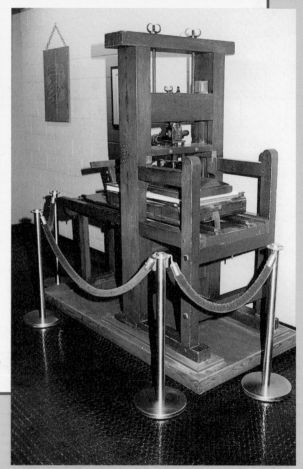

Above: *Historic newspapers line the hallway of the Hartford Courant building.* ***Right:*** *An old-fashioned printing press.*

Many well-known people have been involved with *The Courant* over the years. George Washington once placed an ad to lease part of his Mount Vernon land in *The Courant*. Thomas Jefferson sued *The Courant* for libel (publication of false information about a person) and lost. Mark Twain tried to buy stock in the paper and was rejected.

The *Hartford Courant* printed *The Declaration of Independence* and the *U.S. Constitution* as new documents! Other historic events that made the front page include the beginning of the Civil War, the sinking of the Titanic, the beginning of World War I, and the first moon walk.

The first copy of The Hartford Courant, *then called* The Connecticut Courant.

Copy-Editing and Pagination

At the copy desk, copy editors read stories to make sure they're clear and accurate. They check for grammar and spelling mistakes. Copy editors also write headlines and photo captions. Then layout editors and graphic designers begin to "paginate."

Each newspaper page has many parts that have to be pieced together. Until recently, this process was called "paste-up." In the past, workers called "compositors" cut pieces of type and pasted them onto layout pages.

The Hartford Courant—and many other papers—now have computerized "pagination" systems. This allows workers to paste up pages electronically. Stories, headlines, charts, graphs, photos, and ads are "laid out" into assigned spaces on a computer page. Graphic designers make sure the page is eye-catching, as well as easy to read and understand.

Left: *Copy editors make sure stories are clear and accurate. They work late hours—between 5 P.M. and 1 A.M.*
Opposite: *Newspaper pages are assembled electronically, using a computer "pagination" system.*

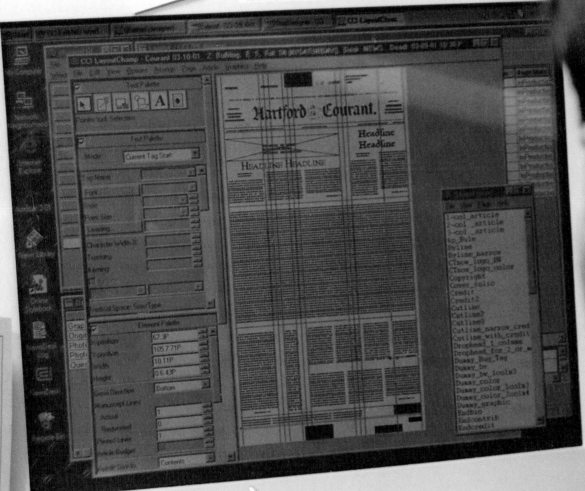

Behind the Scenes

Of the 1,300 employees at The Hartford Courant, only 355 work in the newsroom as reporters, photojournalists, editors, and copy editors. That leaves many other employees who work in other jobs, such as advertising, production, library services, circulation, marketing, finance, newspaper in education, human resources, operations—and, of course, the publisher.

The publisher looks over yesterday's newspaper. The publisher has a big job. He is responsible for decisions that affect both news and the business operations.

*Right: The Newspaper in Education depart-ment shows teachers how to use newspa-pers in class. **Below left:** The letters editor decides which letters from readers appear in the paper each day. **Below right:** A librarian helps staff members find information for stories.*

Advertising

After copy editors paginate the stories and photos, pages are sent electronically to the advertising (ad) department. Here, skilled designers create ads and insert them into the space that's been reserved ahead of time.

Businesses use advertisements to promote products and services to newspaper readers who may be their customers. Readers use classified ads to find homes, jobs, cars, pets, garage sales, and more. Ads are an important part of any newspaper. Advertising can bring in up to 75 percent of the money a newspaper makes.

Managers from the advertising department meet to discuss ways to get more ads for the paper.

THE INSIDE SCOOP

Newspaper advertising accounts for about 22 percent of the nation's total ads.

Platemaking

After all the parts of a page are put together, the page is sent electronically to a machine that creates a negative. This negative is like the negative of a photo snapshot.

The negative and a blank plate are put into a platemaking machine. The plate is coated with light-sensitive chemicals. It also has holes punched into the top.

Light goes through the film and strikes the plate where no black blocks it. That "burns" the image from the negative onto the plate. The plate moves though a processor that washes off the chemicals and puts on a protective coating. The plate is then deliberately bent. The bent edge, along with the holes that were punched earlier, will help the plate hook onto the press.

A worker at the platemaking machine. Each plate runs on the press for about 45 minutes and is used to print about 33,750 pages.

21

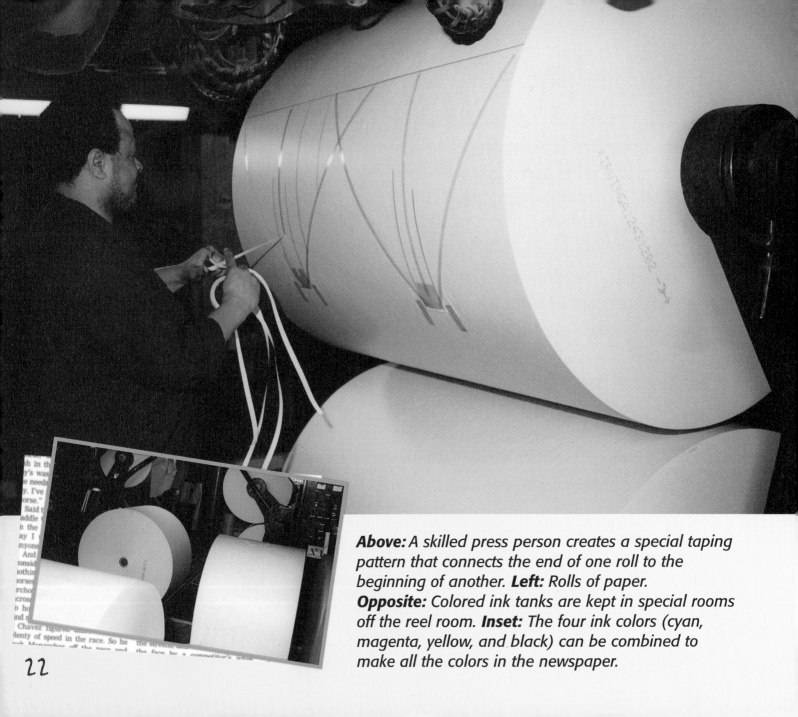

Above: *A skilled press person creates a special taping pattern that connects the end of one roll to the beginning of another.* **Left:** *Rolls of paper.* **Opposite:** *Colored ink tanks are kept in special rooms off the reel room.* **Inset:** *The four ink colors (cyan, magenta, yellow, and black) can be combined to make all the colors in the newspaper.*

The Reel Room

Huge rolls of paper are stored on reels under the pressroom. They are fed up through the pressroom floor onto the presses.

Tanks of red, blue, yellow, and black ink are kept in special rooms. The ink is pumped up into the presses through pipes.

THE INSIDE SCOOP

- The Courant keeps 2-3 days of paper stored in the reel room.
- 40,000 tons of newsprint are used each year. One million pounds of ink are used a year.
- Each full roll of newsprint is about 4 1/2 feet tall, weighs 1,700 lbs., and contains 8 miles of paper! Laid end to end, that much paper would measure 400,000 miles—enough to go around the world 16 times!

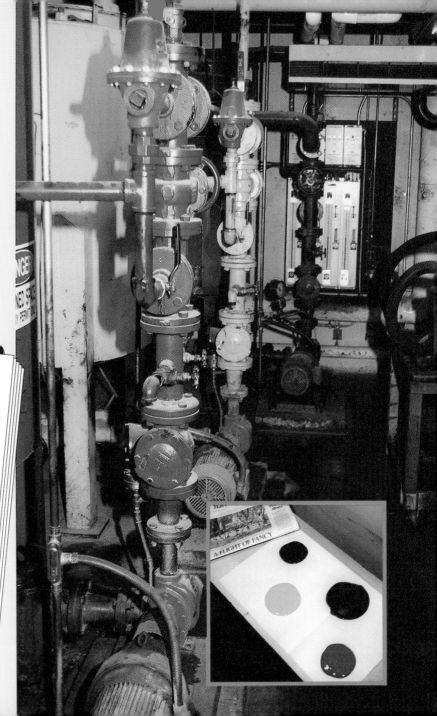

The Pressroom

While most people are getting ready for bed, printers in the pressroom are just starting work. On a typical night, presses begin running at 10 P.M and end by 4 A.M.

Above: *The pressroom.* **Right:** *Plates attached to the press.*

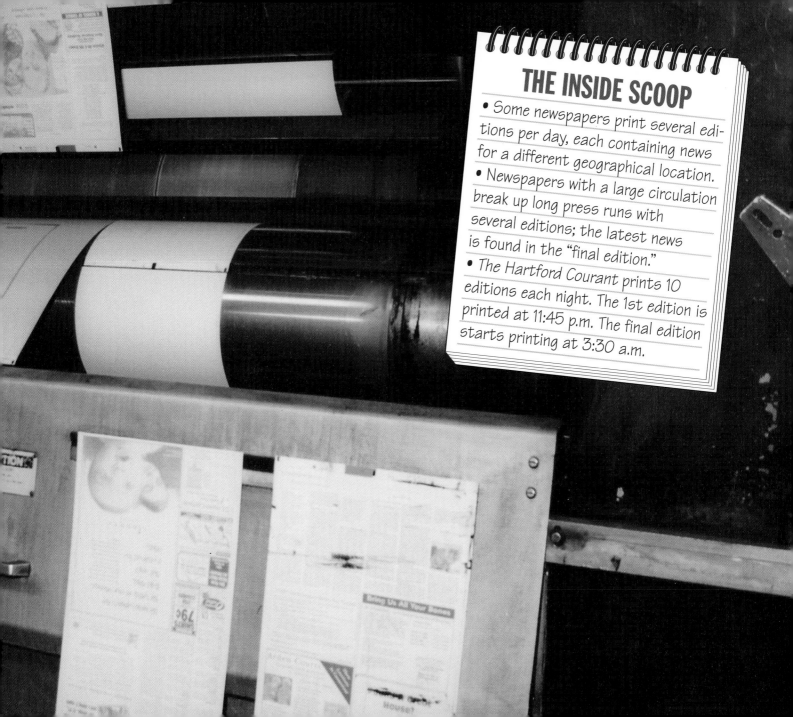

THE INSIDE SCOOP

• Some newspapers print several editions per day, each containing news for a different geographical location.

• Newspapers with a large circulation break up long press runs with several editions; the latest news is found in the "final edition."

• The Hartford Courant prints 10 editions each night. The 1st edition is printed at 11:45 p.m. The final edition starts printing at 3:30 a.m.

Printing the Paper

In the pressroom, operators ink the presses and attach plates. Once the presses begin rolling, sheets are printed, cut, and folded. The folded papers come down a chute, where skilled operators inspect the papers as they come off the press. After inspection, they adjust the press to make the next batch of papers look even better.

Opposite: *Paper moves through the press at high speeds. The pressroom is a loud place. Ear plugs help workers protect their ears.* **Above:** *Press operators inspect papers as they come off the press.*

27

The Mailroom

Next to the pressroom is the mailroom. Papers are sent to the mailroom on conveyors, where they are stacked and bundled. Bundles of papers are then sent down spiral chutes—zooming out the other side at 20-30 miles per hour! They land on more conveyor belts that bring them to the loading area.

Clockwise from top left:
Papers come from the pressroom into the mailroom through this machine. Mailroom workers stack bundles. A truck driver loads a delivery truck.

28

The Online editor works to update the home page of ctnow.com.

Online News

Online "newspapers" represent a new approach to news. The Hartford Courant *produces ctnow.com. This site has more than a dozen newspaper and television partners that contribute information to the site.*

Viewers can find news, sports, weather, and entertainment information on ctnow.com. Just as with the newsprint edition, ads are an important part of the newspaper's online edition.

Online newspapers are an efficient way to update news quickly and often. The ctnow.com site is updated throughout the day.

THE INSIDE SCOOP

Readers view 5-7 million pages per month on ctnow.com

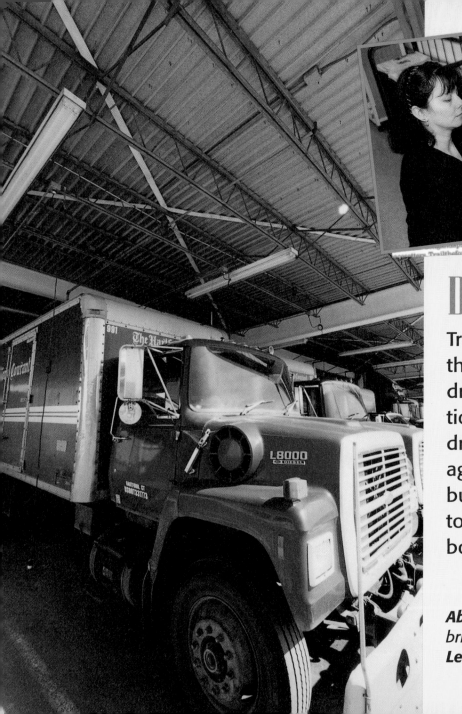

Distribution

Truck drivers quickly deliver the printed newspapers to drop-off points and distribution centers. There, "bulk" drivers, carriers, and vending agents pick up their assigned bundles. These drivers deliver to news dealers, honor boxes, and subscribers.

Above: A worker from circulation brings papers to a local newsstand.
Left: Courant delivery trucks.

NEWSPAPER

More than 75 percent of The Hartford Courant's *newspapers are delivered to homes and businesses. The remaining papers are sold as single-copy sales. These are the papers bought at newsstands, stores, and honor boxes around the state.*

Glossary

Classified ad advertising space that is "classified" into easy-to-use categories, such as jobs, autos, housing, merchandise, and services.

Collate to arrange pages in order.

Editor person responsible for deciding what news goes into the paper.

Libel intentional publication of false information about a person.

Paginate to lay out the pages of the newspaper using a special computer program.

Photojournalist photographer of news.

Press release a specially prepared statement for the press.

Wire service state, national and international news services that provide news and pictures electronically.

For More Information

Books

Greenberg, Keith Elliot. *Photojournalist.* Woodbridge, CT: Blackbirch Press, 1998.

Chambers, Catherine. *Publishing a Newspaper* (Behind Media). Westport, CT: Heinemann Library, 2001.

Graham, Ian, S. *Books and Newspapers* (Communications Close-Up). Chatham, NJ: Raintree/Steck Vaughn, 2000.

Web Sites

The Hartford Courant
Learn more about The Hartford Courant— **www.hartfordcourant.com**

Read stories written by Hartford Courant reporters—**www.ctnow.com**

Index